ISBN-13: 978-0-9989134-0-7
ISBN-10: 0-9989134-0-5

at the moment you trusted in Jesus Christ, you embarked on the most exciting and important adventure you will ever take: the Christian life. If you're reading this book and are new to the Christian life, we rejoice that God has made you alive in Christ. If you've been saved by grace through faith in Jesus, you are now God's workmanship, created to walk the rest of your days in obedience to the Lord (Ephesians 2:1-10). In Christ, you bear a new identity. In him, you are a new creation (2 Corinthians 5:17).

The Bible teaches us that, apart from Christ, we are "filled with all manner of unrighteousness" (Romans 1:29). We are all born as rebels against God, and can do nothing to save ourselves from our fallen state.

"But God," as Paul says in his letter to the Ephesians, "has made you alive in Christ." God showed his love to sinners by sending his perfect Son, Jesus, to bear the wrath you deserved for your sins. He did this so that you could be reconciled to God through Jesus Christ. Once, you were separated from God, but now you're part of "a chosen race, a royal priesthood, a holy nation" (1 Peter 2:9).

The radical transformation you've experienced has made you a disciple of Christ and a member of God's family. To be a Christian is to know and love God as a disciple and as his child, and the primary way God reveals himself to his children is through his Word, the Bible. Though we hope this book is a practical help to you, it can never replace the Bible as your primary authority and aid on this journey. We encourage you to immerse yourself in the pages of Scripture and let them guide you to a deeper understanding of God and an ever-increasing love for him.

In addition to his Word, the Lord has given you another means of discipleship and sanctification: his church. God wants you to live and grow alongside fellow Christians, so let me encourage you to join a local church near you that teaches the Bible. The Bible and the local church will be crucial to your journey through the Christian life because none of us can walk through it alone.

This journey of becoming more like Jesus may take you through suffering, confusion, and sorrows, but God has given you his Word and his church to keep you until the end.

It is our privilege to join you as you embark on this grand adventure called the Christian life. The book in your hands is meant to be a guide to the basics as you set out on your journey. We hope and pray it's a helpful resource for you as you seek to live for the Lord all your days.

JEFF DALRYMPLE,
PRESIDENT OF CROSSINGS MINISTRIES

TABLE OF CONTENTS

PART ONE

Who Is God?

01

The One Who Saves

WHAT IS THE GOSPEL ANYWAY?

BY GREG GILBERT

do you ever wonder what Christians mean when they talk so much about "the gospel?" Every Christian seems to know what they mean when they say that word, and let's be honest: they say it a lot! But what is it? Do you know? Could you explain it to one of your friends?

If you translate the word "gospel" from its original language, it simply means "good news." So when Christians talk about the gospel of Jesus Christ, what they really mean is that they want to tell you some good news about Jesus!

But what exactly is that good news?

What is the gospel?

It can be intimidating when you start thinking about the gospel, because it can seem complicated. But if you see how Jesus and his disciples preached the good news, you realize that it's really not so complicated after all. In fact, the disciples always organized their presentation of the gospel around four questions:

1. Who made us? Who do we answer to?
2. What is our problem? In other words, are we in trouble and why?
3. What is God's solution to that problem? How has he acted to save us from it? And,
4. How do I get to be a part of that solution? What makes this good news for me, and not just for someone else?

Those are the questions they asked. And the answers they gave to those questions were always the same:

1. God made us, and we answer to him.
2. Our problem is our sin — our rebellion against him.
3. God's solution to that problem is salvation through the life, death, and resurrection of Jesus Christ.
4. And we come to be included in that salvation by faith and repentance.

It's really four words: God, man, Christ, and response. So let's think about each.

God, the creator and righteous judge

The beginning of the good news is that God created the heavens and the earth (Genesis 1:1). Since that's true, none of us is our own ruler. We don't make our own rules, and if you're going to understand the gospel, you have to understand that first.

We actually answer to lots of people in our lives, don't we? We're accountable to our parents, teachers, the government, and maybe even a few others like coaches or instructors. But ultimately and most importantly, we're accountable to God. Why? Because he made us.

You were made by God. That means he loves you. But it also means that he owns you. As our maker, God has the right to tell us how to live.

Think about it: if you had to describe God's character in just a few words, what would you say? That he is loving and good? That he is compassionate and forgiving? All that's true. When Moses asked to know God's name, this is what God told him:

> "The Lord, the Lord, a God merciful and gracious, slow to anger, and abounding in steadfast love and faithfulness, keeping steadfast love for thousands, forgiving iniquity and transgression and sin" (Exodus 34:6).

How amazing is that! When God wants to tell us his name — which is really to show us his very heart — what does he say? That he is loving and compassionate, slow to anger, and abounding in love.

But there's something else in that passage that often gets left out, and it's not quite so comforting. Do you know what God says to Moses right after he says that he is compassionate and loving?

We don't make our own rules, and if you're going to understand the gospel, you have to understand that first.

"...but who will by no means clear the guilty."

Read that again, because it blows up about 90 percent of what people today think they know about God. The loving and compassionate God does not leave the guilty unpunished.

If we're going to understand just how awesome the gospel of Jesus Christ is, we have to understand that this loving and compassionate God is also holy and righteous — which means that he is determined never to overlook, ignore, or tolerate sin.

Including our own.

Which brings us to the bad news.

Man, the rebel against God

When God created human beings, he intended for them to live under his rule in perfect joy — worshipping him, obeying him, and living in friendship with him. When Adam and Eve disobeyed God, though, and ate the fruit which God had told them not to eat, their friendship with God was broken. Their minds filled up with selfish thoughts, their eyes went blind to the beauty of God, and their souls became dry and cracked, empty of the spiritual life and joy God gave them in the beginning.

It gets worse, though, because it's not just Adam and Eve who are guilty of sin. The Bible says we all are. Romans 3:23 says, "All have sinned and fall short of the glory of God." And just a few paragraphs earlier it says, "None is righteous, no, not one" (Romans 3:10).

A lot of people think of sin, especially their own, as not all that serious. We think of it as just breaking a little rule here or there, or making a little mistake. It's just not a big deal, we think, and so we wonder why God gets so upset about it.

You have to understand that sin is more than that, though. It's the breaking of a friendship, and even more, it's a rejection of God himself — a rebellion against his rule, his authority, and his right to command those he created. In short, it's a declaration of war against the king of the universe.

Why are we inclined to think our own sin isn't all that bad? How is that different from what the Bible teaches about our sin? To help, read Ephesians 2:1-3 to get an idea of how God views sin.

_____

_____

_____

_____

Once you recognize what sin really is, you start to understand why it's so deadly. Romans 6:23 says, "The wages of sin is death." In other words, the payment we earn for our rebellion against our creator is to die. That's not just talking about physical death, either. It's talking about spiritual death, a forceful separating of our sinful, rebellious selves from the presence of the righteous and holy God.

In fact, Jesus himself said that the final destiny of sinners who don't trust in Jesus to save them is a place of eternal, conscious torment called "Hell," which the Bible describes as a "lake of burning sulfur," a "fiery hell," and a place of "unquenchable fire" (Revelation 20:10; Matthew 9:43).

So that's the Bible's terrifying verdict on us. Not one of us is righteous, not even one. We are all rebels against the king. And we all deserve to be thrown into Hell.

But . . .

Christ's earned obedience becomes yours:

His record of perfect righteousness becomes yours

His death becomes yours (so you don't have to go to Hell)

His resurrection becomes yours

His reward in heaven becomes yours

Jesus Christ, the Savior

When Jesus began to tell his disciples who he was and what he had come to do, this is how he put it: "The Son of Man came not to be served but to serve, and to give his life as a ransom for many" (Mark 10:45). Eventually, the disciples started to understand what he meant. Jesus had come to stand as a substitute for sinners, to live and die in their place so they wouldn't have to fall under the wrath of God themselves.

You see, as Jesus lived his life in perfect obedience to God, he wasn't just doing it for his own sake. He was doing it for his people. He was living life in their place, so that his perfect record could be credited to them as if they had lived that life themselves.

Even more, when Jesus died, he wasn't being punished by God for his own sins (he didn't have any sins to be punished for!). No, he was being punished for his people's sins, in their place. As he hung on the cross at Calvary, Jesus bore all the horrible weight of the sin of God's people. And the curse that God had handed down in Eden — the sentence of death that sin deserves — fell on him. And he died.

But that's not the end of the story. Because Jesus didn't have any sins to die for, death couldn't hold him. Jesus conquered it. And so on the third day, king Jesus rose from the grave.

And this is where the good news of Christianity gets really, really good: the Bible says that when you trust in Jesus to save you, you become united to him. And what he earned for his obedience to God becomes yours, too:

- His record of perfect righteousness becomes yours
- His death becomes yours (so you don't have to go to Hell)
- His reward in heaven becomes yours
- His resurrection becomes yours

That's why the Bible says that to be a Christian is to have "new life," and it's also why it promises that when Jesus comes back, all his people will rise again from the grave to live with him forever.

What incredibly good news this is. But there's still one more question, isn't there? How do I make sure this is good news *for me*?

Our response: faith and repentance

Faith and repentance. This is what marks out those who are Christ's people, or "Christians." In other words, a Christian is one who turns away from sin (repents) and trusts in (has faith in) the Lord Jesus Christ — and nothing else — to save him from sin and the coming judgment.

People often define faith as believing in something you can't prove, but that's not right. It is, biblically speaking, reliance. It's rock-solid, truth-grounded, promise-founded trust in the risen Jesus to save you from sin. The gospel of Jesus Christ calls us to do the very same thing — to put our faith in Jesus, rely on him, and trust him to do what he has promised to do.

We are relying on Jesus to win for us a righteous verdict from God the judge, rather than a guilty one. If God is ever going to count us righteous, he'll have to do it on the basis of something other than our own sinful record. He'll have to do it on the basis of someone else's record, someone who's standing as a substitute for us.

REFLECTION:

One story in the Bible that can help us understand the idea of substitution comes in Genesis 22, the story of Abraham and Isaac. In that story, Abraham is told to sacrifice Isaac, but God supplies a substitute. Read that story and take note of how God spared Isaac's life through the death of another. How does this relate to what Jesus did for his people on the cross?

_____

_____

_____

_____

When you become a Christian, your record of sin and rebellion is credited to Jesus, and he dies for it and wipes it out. And at the same time, the perfect life Jesus lived is credited to us. Then when God looks at us, he doesn't see our record of sin anymore. He sees Jesus' righteousness.

Having faith means trusting Jesus to stand in your place — to live for you the life you should have lived right from the beginning, to die for you the death you deserve because of your sin, and to rise again for you so that, united to him by faith, you will rise right along with him.

At the same time, the Bible says that Jesus' people will be marked by repentance. They'll declare war against their sin. Repentance doesn't mean that we'll immediately stop sinning. But it does mean we'll try. It means we'll declare mortal war against our sin and dedicate ourselves to resisting it by God's power on every front in our lives. After all, to be a Christian is to say, "Jesus is my king now," and sin is our king's mortal enemy.

How to become a Christian

Becoming a Christian is not some difficult, complicated process. There's nothing to earn, no process to go through. The good news is that Jesus has already earned everything you need. What the gospel calls you to do is to turn your heart away from sin and toward Jesus in faith — that is, in trust and reliance. It calls you to come to him and say, "I know I can't save myself, Jesus, so I'm trusting you to do it for me."

And then it calls us to live our lives for his glory — every day until we die and go to be with him in heaven, or until he comes back to get us. What good news that is! And what an awesome way to live your life: saved and forgiven and loved by the risen king Jesus.

RESPONSE:

Now that you've read a chapter about the gospel, use the space below to articulate the good news of the gospel in your own words. One helpful tool can be to use God's own words. To do that, some good verses would be 2 Corinthians 5:21 and Ephesians 2:8-9.

_____

_____

_____

_____

_____

_____

_____

_____

"I have nothing else to rely upon but the fact that Jesus Christ, the Son of God, lived, died, was buried, rose again, went to heaven, and still lives and pleads for sinners at the right hand of God."

-Charles H. Spurgeon

02

The One Who Speaks

BY RANDALL BRELAND

d o you know how God created all things? He used a special tool: his voice. There was nothing until his voice boomed, "Let there be light" (Genesis 1:3). Out of nothing, light penetrated the darkness.

God has finished creating, but he has not finished speaking. The Bible repeats over and over: "God said." The idea that God speaks is a foundation of Christianity and fundamental to your faith. The God that Christians worship is a God who speaks with an all-powerful, cannot-be-resisted, creating voice.

Contrary to what many of your friends may believe, you can hear and understand God's voice today. God speaks today in three ways: his creation, his Word, and his Son, Jesus.

The artist's illustration: God speaks through creation

Pictures of hand-drawn hearts cover my office wall. If you saw these pictures, you would immediately know that I have a daughter who loves pink and loves me. In a similar fashion, you can discern truths about God by looking at creation. Psalm 19:1 confirms that you can learn about God by looking closely at creation: "The heavens declare the glory of God, and the sky above proclaims his handiwork."

Here is some of what God says to you through creation:

He exists

As you gaze upon the breaking ridges of mountains, you understand that someone painted and formed those ridges. The enormous number of stars and the infinite space between them indicates that there is someone out there. Like the stars, the beauty and design of our planet suggests a grand purpose. For example, did you know that the Earth is tilted 23.5 degrees? The tilt of the earth is why there are four seasons, moving weather systems, and large portions of the planet that are habitable by humans. A small change in the tilt would cause much of the world to be too hot or too cold for humans to live.

There are hundreds more evidences of fine-tuning and design such as the beauty and complexity of the human eye or the sheer vastness of the oceans. Through all of these strokes of his brush, God proclaims to every person alive that he exists and that he is the grand designer.

He cares for every living thing

Psalm 104 celebrates how God waters the grass, feeds the animals, and gives food to mankind (Psalm 104:14-23). A morning walk through the woods will reveal thousands of trees, plants, animals, and insects thriving together. In all of these living things, God speaks to you, saying: "I care and provide for everything and everyone in my creation — including you."

Beauty

There's a shape and form to the world that proclaims to all mankind the unfathomable beauty of God. God has made you to recognize that beauty so that he can communicate to you that he is great, glorious, good, and worthy of your trust.

Right and wrong

Every four-year-old proclaims at some point: "Not fair!" Built into every human being is a sense of right and wrong that the Bible calls a conscience. Your conscience is like an internal thermometer that makes you aware of right and wrong. God speaks to you through this common sense of moral fairness. God uses your conscience to encourage you to do what is right and to warn you against what is wrong (see Romans 2:14-16).

Will you stop, look, and listen with your eyes? There are evidences of God everywhere you look.

The friend's letter: God speaks through his Word

When he was sixteen, my father-in-law sent Dwight Eisenhower a letter to encourage him in his presidential campaign. To my father-in-law's delight and surprise, Eisenhower replied with a hand-signed letter. My father-in-law has this letter framed on a wall, because a personal letter from someone so prominent as Eisenhower carries enduring weight and significance.

The Bible is God's letter to us, and is the most significant and enduring letter ever written. It is a collection of sixty-six letters or books from God. Stop and think about how momentous the Bible is for a moment. Has anyone ever written you sixty-six letters? God so desires a relationship with you that he has written all of these, and he wants you to take up and read.

How can you know the Bible is God's Word? Second Timothy 3:16 teaches that "all Scripture is breathed out by God." Through the Holy Spirit, God made sure that his people and his prophets wrote down exactly what he wanted them to write down: "For no prophecy was ever produced by the will of man, but men spoke from God as they were carried along by the Holy Spirit" (2 Peter 1:21).

God is the source of the Bible and the reason Christians give it such value and authority. When you read the Bible, you are reading and hearing God's letter to you — and to all of his people. Since Christians believe that God is true and never lies (see Numbers 23:19; Hebrews 6:18), Christians believe that the Bible is true, without error, and is a trustworthy guide for life. The Bible tells God's people everything they need to know to please and understand him.

His character

You do not have to get out fancy telescopes and peer into the stars to learn about God. All you have to do is open his Word. When Moses asked to see God and to know his ways, God passed before and told Moses who he was:

> "The Lord descended in the cloud and stood with him there, and proclaimed the name of the Lord. The Lord passed before him and proclaimed, 'The Lord, the Lord, a God merciful and gracious, slow to anger, and abounding in steadfast love and faithfulness, keeping steadfast love for thousands, forgiving iniquity and transgression and sin, but who will by no means clear the guilty, visiting the iniquity of the fathers on the children and the children's children, to the third and the fourth generation'" (Exodus 34:5-7).

From creation, you can discern that God is the all-powerful creator. But it is only from his own words that you can learn that he's full of grace, love, justice, and forgiveness.

His will

When God gave Israel his law, it was to teach them how to live in his world. He also gave them a summary of that law called the Ten Commandments. These commandments represent the hundreds of instructions through which God clearly tells you how to live. You do not have to guess how to please God. He has told you!

> When you read the Bible,
> you are reading and hearing
> God's letter to you.

02

God uses his Word to do many things. Read the passages below and reflect on what they say about God's Word and its role in our lives.

2 Timothy 3:16-17
"All Scripture is breathed out by God and profitable for teaching, for reproof, for correction, and for training in righteousness, that the man of God may be complete, equipped for every good work."

_____

_____

_____

_____

Romans 15:4
"For whatever was written in former days was written for our instruction, that through endurance and through the encouragement of the Scriptures we might have hope."

_____

_____

_____

_____

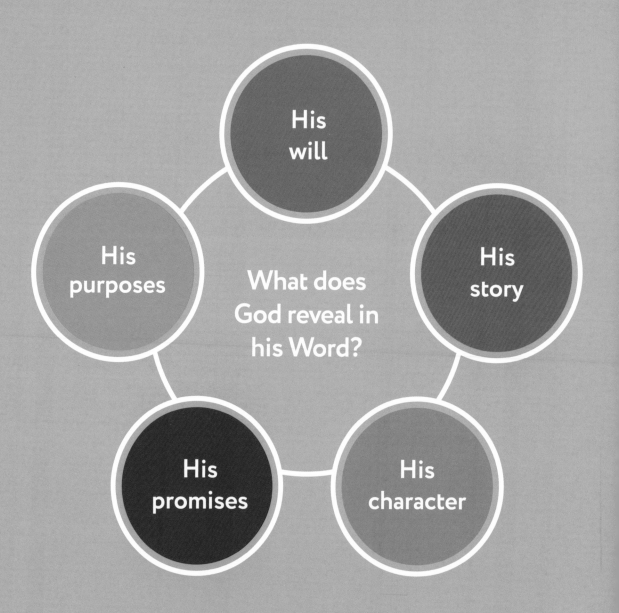

His will

His story

His purposes

What does God reveal in his Word?

His promises

His character

His purposes

First Peter 2:9-10 tells you why God created you and saved you. He creates and saves people so that they would "proclaim the excellencies of him who called you out of darkness into his marvelous light." God created you so that you would make his glory known. The purpose of your life is not to make money, have a family, excel in sports, music, or school. Your purpose in life is to make God and his glory known to others. This may sound unfair until you realize that this is the purpose for which God made you. All of creation — including you, me, and every other human being — is designed to glorify God.

His promises

It is often said: "The Bible is just a bunch of rules." Anyone who has read it cover to cover knows this claim is not true! There are far more promises than there are rules. Second Peter 1:4 says that all believers have been granted "precious and very great promises" through God's power. This is why Paul calls all believers in Jesus "children of the promise" (Galatians 4:28). In the Bible, God promises to love you, care for you, provide for you, be near you, forgive you, have mercy on you, show you favor, save you, raise you from the dead, place you in a new and recreated earth called heaven, and so much more. When you read the Bible, pay attention to God's promises. These promises fuel our faith in him.

His story

The Bible is much more than disconnected quotes, laws, purposes, and promises. All these things are found in the context of a grand story. As you read, you learn that the Bible is a story of how God redeems and saves the entire world from the curse of suffering, sin, and death. When Adam and Eve disobeyed God in the Garden, they brought God's curse on the world and introduced sin and death to mankind. The Bible is the story of how God is restoring the world, turning back the curse, and redeeming his people. It's an invitation to enter the story and take part in it. It's a story about God pursuing you and speaking to you, inviting you into relationship with himself.

Have you ever considered that the Bible is God's very word to you? How should that influence the way you read it and respond to it?

_____

_____

_____

_____

The king's messenger: God speaks through Jesus

How would you feel if the President of the United States sent a personal letter to you like President Eisenhower did to my father-in-law? You would certainly be proud of the letter and sense a special connection to and admiration for the president. Now, imagine that the president came to visit you. If that happened, you would be able to say, "I know the president, and he knows me."

When God sent Jesus, he sent Jesus so that you might know him fully, trust him completely, hear him clearly, and believe him fully. The apostle John reports that Jesus was much more than just a man. Jesus was God in the flesh. Perhaps even more miraculously, John reports that Jesus was the Word of God: "In the beginning was the Word, and the Word was with God, and the Word was God" (John 1:1).

Jesus is the living, walking, and breathing embodiment of everything God has said. Jesus is the ultimate guarantee that what God has said is true. The apostle Paul told the Corinthian church, "...all the promises of God find their Yes in him" (2 Corinthians 1:20).

The entire Bible points you to Jesus as the place to find God, hear God speak, and find life. Through Jesus, God speaks a complete word. The author of Hebrews says that God "has spoken to us by his Son" (Hebrews 1:2), and that Jesus is his final word.

Are you listening?

God has spoken and continues to speak to you today. Creation cries out to you, "God exists!" His word teaches you, "God is loving and just!" Jesus proclaims to you: "You are forgiven. Come, enjoy a relationship with God." Are you listening?

When you have questions, are you willing to sit down and listen to God? There are many questions you will have about God in your Christian life: who are you? What should I do? Can I trust you? How would you respond? Are you real? All of these questions, and many more, are answered in Jesus.

Through the life, death, and resurrection of Jesus, God speaks to us — loudly, clearly, and in full color — and invites us into a relationship with himself today.

God is speaking to you through his creation, through his Word, and ultimately, through Jesus.

Are you listening?

"As the people of God, we believe the word of God can be trusted in every way to speak what is true, command what is right, and provide us with what is good."

- Kevin DeYoung

03

The One
Who Creates

BY KEVIN HALL

"For thus says the Lord, who created the heavens (he is God!), who formed the earth and made it (he established it; he did not create it empty, he formed it to be inhabited!): 'I am the Lord, and there is no other'" (Isaiah 45:18).

great stories in literature usually have riveting first sentences. A good author knows how to reel you into the narrative. In the greatest story ever written — the Bible — the very first verb, or action word, is the word "created." God wants us to know that he is our creator.

The Bible does not try to prove the existence of God; it simply states that God is and that God created. In Genesis 1:1 — the Bible's opening sentence — we read, "In the beginning, God created the heavens and the earth."

Because God is the Creator, he has authority over everything he has made, including humankind. He knows what's best for us. The God of the universe, the God to whom the Bible testifies, is the one who not only created us, but created us with purpose to enjoy and glorify him forever (1 Corinthians 10:13).

QUESTIONS:

In addition to being the creator of the universe, God is also the sustainer of all things. What do these verses say about God's continued relationship to his creation?

Acts 17:25
God "gives to all mankind life and breath and everything."

Hebrews 1:3
Jesus "upholds the universe by the word of his power."

_____

_____

_____

_____

Creation of the universe

What comes into your mind when you think about God? One man said your answer to this question is the most important thing about you! One of the answers that comes to mind is that God is big, and a part of this bigness comes from the reality that God is the creator.

Another question we can ask is, "What does God's creation tell us about him?" As we look at the creation around us, we can see the handiwork and beauty of God the creator. I'm originally from California, and when I think of the Pacific Ocean, or Yosemite National Park, or a sunset, or even the color of a cardinal against the backdrop of the snow here in Kentucky, I am amazed at the beauty of God in his creation.

God's creation of the world and the universe in which we live is called "general revelation," meaning that the creation reveals something about God to us. We see this idea clearly in Psalm 19:1, which says that "the heavens declare the glory of God, and the sky above proclaims his handiwork." God's creation says something about God. We can learn about God from what we see around us, though we can't learn everything. Ultimately, it is the truth of his Word as we see it in the Bible that reveals to us everything we need to know about the creator and his creation, including you and me.

QUESTIONS:

Take a moment to consider the world around you — the sky, the people, the trees. Now consider the world at large — the mountains, the oceans, the stars. What do these things communicate about God?

_____

_____

_____

_____

_____

The uncreated one

Have you ever thought about what makes God, God? Simply put, God is not only the creator, he is also the only one who is self-existent. God has always existed from eternity past to eternity future. He is eternal.

When God revealed himself to Moses, he introduced himself as "I am who I am" (Exodus 4:14). That may seem like a strange way for someone to introduce himself, but it points to God's self-existence. God has always been, and will always be! Try to wrap your mind around that truth. We are dealing with a God much bigger than anything we can imagine.

You can see that there's a significant difference between who God is and who we are. We were created and are not self-existent. Unlike you and me, God has no origin date. Mine was a spring day in 1969, but God has always been. He alone is uncreated.

Created in God's image

Up until the fifth day of creation, God ended each day with "and it was good." But after the sixth day, when God had finished his creative work, he declared it all to be "very good" (Genesis 1:31). This distinction of being "very good" comes just after God made Adam and Eve: "So God created man in his own image, in the image of God he created him; male and female he created them" (Genesis 1:27). Humans made in God's image are the pinnacle of God's creation. He saved the best for last.

What does it mean to be made in the image of God? There is something special in this wording, for when God says that we're made in his image, it means there's a likeness of God in us. God's relationship with humankind is unique because no other creature bears God's image.

The words for "image" and "likeness" mean that there is something similar to the original, like how the Abraham Lincoln monument bears the image of the real Lincoln. The similarity between God and humankind consists of our ability to reason (to think through things critically), where we have an intellect, a will, and emotions. Being created this way also means we're made to be creative and to exercise dominion and care over God's creation.

God

created the universe

has authority over all things

is self-existent

is eternal

created mankind in his image

A distorted image

The entrance of sin into the world changes things. The image of God in us is now corrupted, but it's still there. For example, in Genesis 9:6, which comes after the fall, God states, "Whoever sheds the blood of man, by man shall his blood be shed, for God made man in his own image."

This reality is also stated in the New Testament, where James writes that all people, saved and unsaved "are made in the likeness of God" (James 3:9).

We still bear the likeness of God, but not perfectly. We've lost our purity and our minds are corrupted, which in turn affects our speech and actions.

Although the image is distorted, we still retain the image of God, and we're still his representatives on the earth. We can see this in the relationships we have, in a painter's creativity on a canvas, an author's mastery of language, and a musician's skill, as well as in the work of science and industry and human ingenuity.

But sin is still a reality, and because of sin, we need this image to be restored, to be made right. God gave the solution to this problem when he sent his Son, Jesus Christ.

The Bible describes Christ as the second Adam, because Jesus was perfect in obedience where the first Adam was not. When Adam faced temptation, he fell. When Christ faced temptation, he honored God and never sinned. Christ was the true and full image of the invisible God (Colossians 1:15; Romans 5:12-21).

Jesus died in our place, taking our sin upon himself, and then rose from the dead on the third day victorious over sin and death. This truth changes everything, so that in Christ we can be transformed into a new creation with a new heart (2 Corinthians 5:17). God makes us alive spiritually and begins the process of recovering God's image.

RESPONSE:

Read Romans 5:12-21. How did Jesus' life and ministry relate to the life of Adam? How were they different?

_____

_____

_____

_____

_____

_____

_____

"It would be good for us to reflect on our likeness to God more often. It will probably amaze us to realize that when the Creator of the universe wanted to create something 'in his image,' something more like himself than all the rest of creation, he made us. This realization will give us a profound sense of dignity and significance as we reflect on the excellence of all the rest of God's creation: the starry universe, the abundant earth, the world of plants and animals, and the angelic kingdoms are remarkable, even magnificent. But we are more like our Creator than any of these things. We are the culmination of God's infinitely wise and skillful work of creation. Even though sin has greatly marred that likeness, we nonetheless now reflect much of it and shall even more as we grow in likeness to Christ."
-Wayne Grudem

03

God's authority over creation

Because God made the heavens and the earth (Genesis 1:1), he is the owner of all things: "the earth is the Lord's, and the fullness thereof, the world and all those who dwell therein" (Psalm 24:1). Being the owner and maker of all things means he has authority over all things.

These truths are important to note because, as sinners, we do not care for God's authority. We fight against the truth of his authority. But when we realize who God is — not only in his authority, but also in his holiness, grace, faithfulness, goodness, love, mercy, and wisdom — we will be drawn to him in all his beauty.

In Psalm 16, David wrote, "You make known to me the path of life; in your presence, there is fullness of joy; at your right hand are pleasures forevermore" (Psalm 16:11). A few centuries later, Jesus said, "I came that they may have life and have it abundantly." (John 10:10). God made us, and he made us to have joy in knowing him. We are created for him, who is our good — period. So instead of being confining to us, God's authority is good news because he knows what is best for us as people created in his image.

One day he will make things right in a new creation where paradise lost will be regained. It is in the new creation, as God restores all things, that we will continue to grow in our understanding of who he is. We, along with all creation, wait eagerly for that moment (Romans 8:18-23).

"When we realize that God created us to glorify him, and when we start to act in ways that fulfill that purpose, then we begin to experience an intensity of joy in the Lord that we have never before known."

-Wayne Grudem

The One Who Is with Us

BY PAUL CHITWOOD

04

I f you've given your life to Jesus, having repented of your sins and confessed him as your Lord, the Bible says you are saved. Saved from what? You have been saved from your sin and the spiritual consequences of your sin. What are the consequences of sin? The Bible teaches us that sin brought death into the world, separates us from God for time and eternity, and keeps us from living out the purpose for which God made us. Needless to say, you are in a much different place in life and have a much different future since you have decided to follow Jesus.

Sometimes we question whether we are truly saved and we're uncertain we are going to heaven. Questions like that can arise when we aren't sure God is hearing our prayers, when we feel alone, when something terrible has happened to us or to someone we love, or when we've done something wrong. In other words, circumstances and feelings can cause us to wonder whether we are saved.

If that happens to you, know that you are not alone. Most of us have had feelings and questions like that. Because God knows us and loves us, he wants to help us through those times. And he definitely doesn't want us to be unsure of what is most important in our lives, that is, whether we belong to him.

In the Bible, God has given us some assurances he wants us to have so we don't spend our lives wondering whether we are saved. In short, God has promised to preserve and be with his people. These promises are true regardless of our circumstances and regardless of how we may feel at a given moment in time. What does it mean for God to preserve and be with his people?

> ## If you are a follower of Jesus, God has adopted you and nothing will ever change that.

God won't give you up

One of my children is adopted. She was ten months old when God brought her into our family, but the adoption process started even before she was born. That process involved a lot of legal paperwork, a long waiting period, and adoption fees. But finally, on a beautiful day in June, the adoption was finalized and she became my daughter. I love her more than I love my own life and would never give her up. I am her father. Nothing will ever change that.

Galatians 4:4-5 states,
"But when the fullness of time had come, God sent forth his Son, born of woman, born under the law, to redeem those who were under the law, so that we might receive adoption as sons."

Many years passed after the prophets announced the coming Messiah, but finally the time for his coming arrived. The Bible teaches us that Jesus lived a perfect life, never committing a single sin. Then, he willingly gave up his life to pay the price of our sin. In so doing, Jesus fulfilled God's law, paid for our adoption in full by his death on the cross, and redeemed us. Because of what he has done, we are now God's sons and daughters. God is our Father and he will never give his children up.

In John 10:28-29, Jesus is talking about his followers when he states:
"I give them eternal life, and they will never perish, and no one will snatch them out of my hand. My Father, who has given them to me, is greater than all, and no one is able to snatch them out of the Father's hand."

I recall the time I met Reggie White, a professional football player and minister. During his career, White was one of the most intimidating defensive players in the NFL, earning him the nickname "the Minister of Defense." What I remember most about our meeting was shaking his hand. I'm over six feet tall and can palm a basketball, but shaking hands with Reggie White made me feel like a little kid. He was a big man, but his hands were huge. He had a grip of steel. If Reggie White grabbed hold of you, you weren't getting away.

How much stronger is the God of the universe, with his unlimited power? Who could take you away from him? If you are a follower of Jesus, God has adopted you and nothing will ever change that.

If God has given you eternal life, he won't take it back

Have you ever given a very special gift to someone you loved and then asked for it back? Probably not. That isn't a gift; it's a loan.

In John 3:16, Jesus states,
"For God so loved the world that he gave his only Son, that whoever believes in him should not perish but have eternal life."

God gave his Son to provide for our salvation. The salvation that God, in his great mercy, has given us in Jesus, isn't a loan. It's the most wonderful gift that could ever be given, and it comes to us because of God's great love as a gift of grace. Grace is favor that we receive even though we haven't earned it.

You may wonder, "What if I do something bad? Couldn't I lose my salvation?" Remember, you aren't saved because you did things that were good. You are saved through grace because of God's great love. That is to say, our salvation isn't based upon works. The Bible makes that clear in Ephesians 2.

In Ephesians 2:8-9, the apostle Paul states,
"For by grace you have been saved through faith. And this is not your own doing; it is the gift of God, not a result of works, so that no one may boast."

If salvation isn't based upon works but is a gift of God's grace, then we don't have to worry about "slipping up" and losing it. Salvation is God's gift to you. He won't take it back.

QUESTIONS:

Since salvation is a gift and not a loan, what does this mean for your security and assurance?

_____

_____

_____

God is with you

Describing God isn't easy. In fact, most of the words we use to describe God fall short of communicating how indescribably wonderful and amazing he is. One word we use to describe God is omnipresent. That means God is present everywhere, all of the time.

The psalmist asked,
"Where shall I go from your Spirit? Or where shall I flee from your presence?" (139:7)

In the book of Romans, the apostle Paul asks,
"Who shall separate us from the love of Christ? Shall tribulation, or distress, or persecution, or famine, or nakedness, or danger, or sword?" (8:35).

He concludes,
"I am sure that neither death nor life, nor angels nor rulers, nor things present nor things to come, nor powers, nor height nor depth, nor anything else in all creation, will be able to separate us from the love of God in Christ Jesus our Lord" (Romans 8:38-39).

The Bible teaches that God is everywhere, all of the time, and that God is especially near to his people. Jesus said, "For where two or three are gathered in my name, there am I among them" (Matthew 18:20).

In Hebrews 13:5, the Bible promises God will never leave us nor forsake us. If God is everywhere, all the time and you, now that you are saved, belong to him, surely he is with you.

Four promises from God

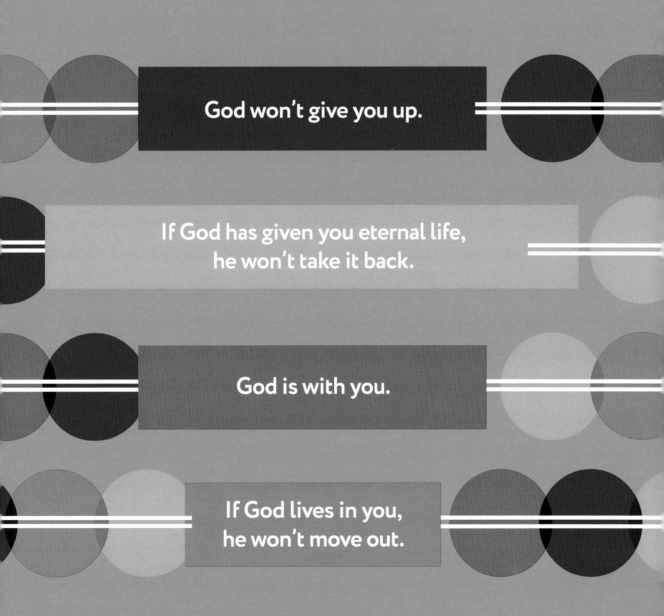

God won't give you up.

If God has given you eternal life,
he won't take it back.

God is with you.

If God lives in you,
he won't move out.

Why is it important and comforting to know that God is with us? How might that influence your day-to-day life?

_____

_____

_____

_____

If God lives in you, he won't move out

Have you ever moved from one house or apartment to another? You may have been happy about the move or you may have been sad but, either way, you kept on living. Has your heart ever moved out of your body? Not unless you have had a heart transplant. Otherwise, you wouldn't be alive.

When you trusted in Jesus as your Savior and acknowledged him as your Lord, something amazing happened. Jesus, through the Holy Spirit, became an inseparable part of your life. The apostle Paul explains it like this in Galatians 2:20,

"I have been crucified with Christ. It is no longer I who live, but Christ who lives in me. And the life I now live in the flesh I live by faith in the Son of God, who loved me and gave himself for me."

Salvation not only brings changes like forgiveness of sin and a new eternal destiny, it also means that, through the Holy Spirit, Jesus now lives with you and in you. In God's eyes, your life is now connected intimately and permanently to his Son, Jesus. Jesus lives in you.

Another place the Bible affirms that Jesus is in the life of every person who has placed their faith in him is in 2 Corinthians 13:5. Paul states,

"Examine yourselves, to see whether you are in the faith. Test yourselves. Or do you not realize this about yourselves, that Jesus Christ is in you?"

When you read the Bible, you will notice that the book is filled with God's promises. And God does not break his promises. Everything God says that he'll do, he either has done it or will do it. God has promised to be with his people, and one of the last things Jesus said to his disciples before ascending was, "I am with you always, to the end of the age" (Matthew 28:20).

So the real question isn't, "Is Jesus still in me or with me?" The real question is, "Have you placed your faith in Jesus?" If so, then he lives in you. And, rest assured, he won't move out.

"Fear not,
for I am with you;
be not dismayed,
for I am your God;
I will strengthen you,
I will help you,
I will uphold you with my
righteous right hand."
-Isaiah 41:10

The Three-in-One

BY JAMES M. HAMILTON JR. AND MATT DAMICO

you were made to know God. This is one of life's great truths, that God made you with the capacity to know him. In fact, human beings are most fully human when they know God, when they put all their trust in him, and when they live to his glory.

In order to glorify God, you've got to think right thoughts about him. You've got to know the God of the Bible. As Christians, the most distinct and foundational reality about God is that he is a Trinity. He is three and he is one, and there is none like him.

The one and only

It's not uncommon to hear someone make the claim that Muslims and Christians worship the same God. They'll say that the "Allah" of the Qur'an and the God of the Bible are the same being.

If someone asks you, "Do Muslims and Christians worship the same God," here's your answer: No, they do not. And the reason is that Muslims reject the reality of who God is. They deny the notion that God is triune (three-in-one).

An old Christian catechism has two significant questions on this point:

Question: Are there more Gods than one?
Answer: There is only one living and true God.

Question: How many persons are there in the Godhead?
Answer: There are three persons in the Godhead: the Father, the Son, and the Holy Spirit, and these three are one God, the same in essence, equal in power and glory.

Muslims would answer the first question the same way Christians would. But they would vehemently disagree with the second. They reject the Trinity. Christians, however, believe that the Bible teaches that there is one God, but that this one God exists as three persons. How can this be?

To answer this question, we will first consider the Bible's claims that Father, Son, and Holy Spirit are God. From there we will consider how these three can be one.

What the Bible teaches

The Father

This point is hardly worth making. The evidence that the Father is God is everywhere. In much of the New Testament, the Father is simply referred to as "God." Even so, here are a couple examples:

> "Grace, mercy, and peace will be with us, from God the Father and from Jesus Christ the Father's Son, in truth and love" (2 John 1:3:).

> "Then comes the end, when [Christ] delivers the kingdom to God the Father after destroying every rule and every authority and power" (1 Corinthians 15:24).

The Son

> "In the beginning was the Word, and the Word was with God, and the Word was God" (John 1:1). Here, "the Word" refers to Jesus.

> "For in [Christ] the whole fullness of deity dwells bodily" (Colossians 2:9).

> "To them belong the patriarchs, and from their race, according to the flesh, is the Christ, who is God over all, blessed forever. Amen" (Romans 9:5).

The Spirit

"But Peter said, 'Ananias, why has Satan filled your heart to lie to the Holy Spirit ... You have not lied to man but to God'" (Acts 5:3-4).

Notice how "the Holy Spirit" is referred to as "God." When Ananias lied to the Spirit, he lied to God.

In Mark 3, Jesus is recorded as saying that "whoever blasphemes against the Holy Spirit never has forgiveness, but is guilty of an eternal sin." Blasphemy in the Bible is only ever against God.

> "The Spirit searches everything, even the depths of God" (1 Corinthians 2:10). Who could search the depths of God except God himself?

All Together

There are also places in the New Testament where the Father, Son, and Spirit are mentioned together, placing them on equal footing with one another:

> "Jesus said, 'Go therefore and make disciples of all nations, baptizing them in the name of the Father and of the Son and of the Holy Spirit'" (Matthew 28:18-20).

> "The grace of the Lord Jesus Christ and the love of God and the fellowship of the Holy Spirit be with you all" (2 Corinthians 13:14).

REFLECTION:

The Trinity can be a complex and difficult teaching. It shows us that God is not like us. His greatness and complexity should draw us to worship. Read these verses and write out how it informs your view of God.

"For my thoughts are not your thoughts, neither are your ways my ways, declares the Lord. For as the heavens are higher than the earth, so are my ways higher than your ways and my thoughts than your thoughts" (Isaiah 55:8-9).

_____

_____

_____

_____

_____

_____

_____

_____

All three members of the godhead are

Omniscient ——————— They each know everything.

Holy ——————— They each want only what is right and good.

Loving ——————— They each feel the same devotion and compassion.

How can three be one?

With all this evidence, there is still much to sort through. How do we make sense of the biblical teaching that there is one God, and that he exists in three persons?

When we talk about the Trinity, it can be helpful to clarify what the Bible doesn't teach, and what Christians therefore don't believe:

Christians don't believe there are three Gods.

Nor do Christians believe that one God manifests himself in three different ways, as though God revealed himself as Father for a while, then as Jesus for a time, then as the Spirit. There are three distinct persons who share one divine nature.

Christians do not hold to three natures in God. There is one divine nature shared by the three persons of the Godhead.

Nor do Christians hold to one person in God. There are three persons in the Godhead.

Christians have devoted much thought to these realities over the centuries, and there are some important concepts that have developed as ways to help us think it all through.

One will in God

The first concept is that there is one will in God. Saying that there is one will in God is simply saying that the Father, Son, and Spirit are in absolute and perfect agreement with one another. Even the closest allies among people will disagree occasionally. Friends will argue, and families sometimes need space from one another. Not so in the Godhead. The Father, Son, and Spirit have the same purpose, and they are in complete agreement on how to bring about that purpose.

All three members of the Godhead are omniscient. They each know everything.

All three members of the Godhead are holy. They each want only what is right and good.

All three members of the Godhead are loving. They each feel the same devotion and compassion.

The result of all this is that in all things, the Father, the Son, and the Holy Spirit are in perfect agreement with one another.

If the Father, Son, and Holy Spirit did not share the single divine will, it would result from some deficiency in one of them. But the Father, Son, and Holy Spirit are complete in every perfection, and as a result they are united in all things, including their will.

If the three members of the Godhead do not share the same will, they are not one God.

Eternal relations of origin

The second concept is eternal relations of origin. The word "origin" speaks to where something comes from. Where does God come from? He doesn't. He has always been. So when we say "origin" in relation to God, we're not talking about where God came from. Instead, we're trying to distinguish the Father from the Son and the Spirit. The challenge is to say as much as the Bible says and no more.

The Bible refers to God as Father, and we also read of the Son referred to as the "only-begotten" of the Father. In some mysterious way that is beyond our comprehension, the Father has been begetting the Son from eternity past. Jesus seems to speak to this in John 5:26 when he says, "as the Father has life in himself, so he has granted the Son to have life in himself."

05

The Father has always had life in himself, and so has the Son. So it shouldn't be a surprise to see that he grants life to us, too. Whether you're aware if it or not, God keeps your heart beating and your lungs pumping. How can this truth change the way you pray and think about your daily life?

_____

_____

_____

_____

If there was a time when the Son did not have life in himself, then there was a time when the Son was not everything the Father is. The only satisfying conclusion is that the Father has always been granting to the Son to have life in himself. This is the kind of thing meant when people speak of the Son as the one eternally begotten of the Father. Clearly, this is different than human begetting.

The Father and the Son can be distinguished from one another by the fact that the Father begets and the Son is begotten.

Similarly, Jesus speaks of the way that he will give the Spirit to the disciples in John 14-16, and in John 15:26 Jesus speaks of the Spirit "who proceeds from the Father." Since Jesus also gives the Spirit in these passages — earlier in the verse he says that he himself will send the Spirit — theologians say that the Spirit proceeds from both the Father and the Son.

The Father begets. The Son is begotten. And the Spirit proceeds from the Father and the Son. This is the way it has always been: these "eternal relations of origin" have always been true of the three persons of the Godhead. This is how we know the difference of the Father from the Spirit and the Son.

Inseparable operations

When people speak of inseparable operations, our third concept, what they mean is that every member of the Godhead is involved in everything God does. The Father does not go off as a maverick and do something without the Son and the Spirit. The Son and the Spirit don't go it alone on some private project of their own, either.

Every member of the Godhead is involved in everything God does.

This has been true from the very beginning. Consider the creation of the universe:

The Bible says that God created everything: "In the beginning, God created the heavens and the earth" (Genesis 1:1). In the very next verse, Moses tells us that "the Spirit of God was hovering over the face of the waters." Then, the New Testament describes Jesus as the Son "through whom also [the Father] created the world" (Hebrews 1:2). In the act of creation, the Father spoke the universe into being through the Son, with the Spirit present, too. Every person of the Godhead was involved.

Another example comes in Christ's death for sin. When Jesus the Son shed his blood for sinners, it was a Trinitarian act. We see this in Hebrews 9, where the author says that Christ "through the eternal Spirit offered himself without blemish to God" (Hebrews 9:14). The Son offered himself to the Father through the Spirit.

Trinitarian plunge

To plunge into the doctrine of the Trinity is to dive in the pool's deepest end. We were made to know God, but we will never know him fully. Christians will spend all eternity growing in the knowledge of God, and we'll never know it all.

So I hope this is just the beginning of a life-long endeavor to know God. The more deeply you know him, the more fully you will worship him. The apostle Paul is a good example in this. In his letter to the church in Rome, he goes deep into the things of God. But this doesn't dull his devotion. On the contrary, his response is doxology. And what better way could there be for us to end our Trinitarian thoughts:

"Oh, the depth of the riches and wisdom and knowledge of God! How unsearchable are his judgments and how inscrutable his ways!
'For who has known the mind of the Lord,
or who has been his counselor?'
'Or who has given a gift to him
that he might be repaid?'
For from him and through him and to him are all things. To him be glory forever. Amen" (Romans 11:33-36).

REFLECTION:

The Bible's teaching on the Trinity can be a lot to sort through. What have been the biggest takeaways from this chapter for you?

_____

_____

_____

_____

_____

_____

"To know the Trinity is to know God, an eternal and personal God of infinite beauty, interest, and fascination. The Trinity is a God we can know, and forever grow to know better."

-Michael Reeves

PART TWO

Who Am I?

06

A Child of God

BY MATT DAMICO

06

"Who am I?"

try answering that question. Seriously, when you try to define yourself, what comes to your mind first? Do you think of yourself mainly as an athlete, or a musician, or a sibling, son, daughter, or something else? It's a fundamental question, and a lot of people are confused about how to answer. Maybe you're confused, too.

Thankfully, the Bible has a lot to say about who Christians are. If you've put your faith in Jesus and committed yourself to following him, you don't need to be confused.

In order to develop a healthy, biblical self-understanding, you've got to begin by looking away from yourself. You've got to start with God. That might seem counter-intuitive, but the first step toward knowing yourself is knowing God. We're made in God's image, so everything we learn about him informs our self-understanding, too.

In addition to that, we're creatures that God has made, we live in a world he has made, at a time he appointed, in a family we didn't choose. In other words, everything about us is true because God made it that way, so our identity is first and foremost about who we are in relation to him.

Knowing this much, let's consider again our question, "who am I?" For Christians, another way to ask the question is to ask "what is a Christian?"

To help us answer, I'm going to turn to J.I. Packer, who answers this question beautifully:

"'What is a Christian?' The question can be answered in many ways, but the richest answer I know is that a Christian is one who has God as Father."

A Christian is one who has God as Father. That's who you are, and it's worth exploring more deeply.

Adopted

Nobody is born as part of God's family. We're all born into a messed up, sinful world with messed up, sinful hearts. We were strangers to God, homeless and orphaned by our sin.

The Bible says that, before trusting in Christ, we were:

"darkened in [our] understanding, alienated from the life of God" (Ephesians 4:18).

"by nature children of wrath, like the rest of mankind" (Ephesians 2:3).

Prior to knowing Jesus as Lord, everyone is separated from God. And yet, God sought us out and made us his own.

He did this by sending his Son to live, die, and rise again for us. We deserved to die, but Christ died in our place. So not only did God the Father save unworthy people, he paid the highest cost to do so by crushing his own Son.

One of my friends adopted a baby boy from a country in Africa a number of years ago. Shortly after that little boy was born, he was completely abandoned, left either to die or be discovered by someone else. He was mercifully found and brought to an orphanage. Now, that little boy has parents who love him dearly, provide for him, keep him safe, and teach him the gospel. That boy now shares their name. He was lost and abandoned, but his parents came looking for him and made him their own.

That's the glory of adoption, and that's precisely what the Father does for his children. He finds us and changes us forever. The apostle Paul says that "God sent forth his Son ... so that we might receive adoption as sons" (Galatians 4:4–5). If you have trusted in Christ, it's because the Father has gone to incredible lengths to make you his own.

You were not a child of God when you were born. You become a child of God when you were born again, so that "in Christ Jesus you are all sons of God, through faith" (Galatians 3:26). As Christians, we share Christ's name, his blood is our blood, and his Father is our Father.

What are some life changes that happen to a child who's adopted? How do those things correlate to the spiritual adoption that we receive as Christians?

Beloved

The New Testament uses a range of images to describe the identity of Christians: we're members of the body of Christ, sheep in a flock, part of Christ's bride, living stones in God's temple, and so on. All of these images are true and informative.

But the idea that we're children of God is unique because we share this status with Jesus. We're adopted sons and daughters, and Jesus is the Son of God, the perfect image of his Father.

This has some too-good-to-be-true implications for us. To start, God the Father loves all of his children the way he loves his only begotten Son. The Father's love for us is so unbreakable that nothing "in all creation will be able to separate us from the love of God in Christ Jesus our Lord" (Romans 8:38). Because we are in Christ, the Father looks on us with the same love, commitment, and pleasure. We could never be worthy of that love. Christ has earned it for us.

Heirs

A few years ago it came out that Bill Gates and Warren Buffett – two of the world's richest men – would not be leaving massive inheritances for their children. Their motives are good: they want their children to earn their own way.

But that's not how the Father operates. He's so generous that he shares Christ's inheritance with us. As God's perfect Son, Jesus was a qualified heir, and he earned his inheritance: he's the "heir of all things" (Hebrews 1:2). He's received a kingdom, and all authority in heaven and on earth is his. We earned none of it, and yet we will share in it. Look at all the New Testament has to say about this:

"The Spirit himself bears witness with our spirit that we are children of God, and if children, then heirs—heirs of God and fellow heirs with Christ" (Romans 8:16–17).

"Those who are called may receive the promised eternal inheritance" (Hebrews 9:15).

God, in his great mercy, "has caused us to be born again … to an inheritance that is imperishable, undefiled, and unfading, kept in heaven for you" (1 Peter 1:3–4).

What is this inheritance? It's all that Christ earned. Through his victory over sin and death, he received an eternal kingdom. As co-heirs, we receive eternal citizenship in that kingdom. The Father adopts sinners into his family, loves them as his own, and gives them the unfathomable inheritance of eternal life.

Every blessing we enjoy in this life is a taste of the eternal inheritance we're going to receive. What are some of those blessings of the inheritance that we enjoy now?

_____

_____

_____

_____

Protected

When I was growing up, my family said this prayer before dinner every night: "God is great, God is good. Let us thank him for our food. Amen."

As a kid, I neither understood nor appreciated the difference between God being "great" and God being "good." It just sounded like two ways of saying the same thing. I was wrong.

To say "God is great" is to describe the power, the immensity, and the total uniqueness of God. Nothing compares to him, and nobody is like him. To say "God is good" is to describe the way God does what he does. Everything he does is good. He's kind, wise, and loving.

Now put those things together: the God who is great is also good. The one powerful enough to mold the planets is willing to listen to your prayers. If you're a Christian, your Father in heaven is the most powerful person in the universe – because he made the universe! And he's on your side.

As you go through life, you'll face hundreds of situations that make you nervous or afraid. In those moments, remember that your Father is with you, and there's no fear that he can't overwhelm. When you read your Bible, take note of how often God tells his people "fear not" or "do not fear." God knows there are fear-inducing situations. He doesn't say our lives will be easy, but he's greater than whatever we might face.

And God promises to use every single thing for our good. Romans 8:28 says that "for those who love God all things work together for good." God won't let anything happen to you that isn't ultimately good for you.

If God wasn't good, he would be a terrifying force. If he wasn't great, he'd be a well-intended but ill-equipped God. But thankfully, our God and Father is great and good. And he is for us.

> If God wasn't good, he would be a terrifying force. If he wasn't great, he'd be a well-intended but ill-equipped God. But thankfully, our God and Father is great and good. And he is for us.

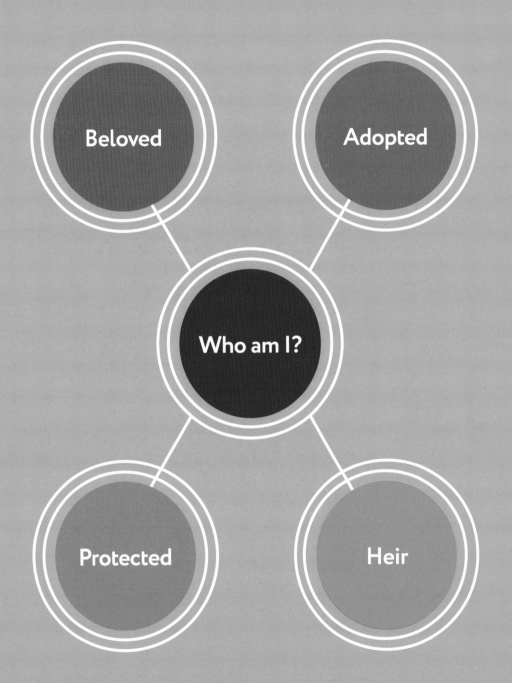

Walk and talk

Belonging to God's family brings joy and privilege, and it comes with responsibility. The Bible says that God expects some things from his children.

God calls us to live by his standards.

It's his family, and he sets the house rules. The apostle Peter tells Christians that, "As obedient children, do not be conformed to the passions of your former ignorance, but as he who called you is holy, you also be holy in all your conduct, since it is written, 'You shall be holy, for I am holy'" (1 Peter 1:14–16).

As God's children, everything we do reflects our Father. For the sake of illustration, let's say you play basketball for your school, and at one of your games you do something really foolish like trip an opponent or throw a temper tantrum at the referee. Without a doubt, this episode reflects poorly on you. But it also reflects poorly on your parents and your school, because you represent both.

That's how it is in the Christian life. What we do reflects our Father, and disobedience is not a true reflection of who he is. Jesus told his followers that they should walk in obedience, so that the watching world "may see your good works and give glory to your Father who is in heaven" (Matthew 5:16).

> **What we do reflects our Father, and disobedience is not a true reflection of who he is.**

06

We're invited to pray to our Father.

It's significant that Jesus taught his disciples to pray the words, "Our Father." Only God's children can use those words. So take advantage of this incredible relationship you have, that you can call upon the Almighty as Father.

Jesus encouraged his disciples by comparing God the Father to earthly fathers:

> "Which one of you, if his son asks him for bread, will give him a stone? Or if he asks for a fish, will give him a serpent? If you then, who are evil, know how to give good gifts to your children, how much more will your Father who is in heaven give good things to those who ask him" (Matthew 7:9–11).

God wants to hear from you, and he enjoys answering your prayers. He loves to give gifts. Pray to him.

Let's revisit our question from the beginning of the chapter: "Who am I?" It's my prayer that you can answer that question with biblical clarity and confidence for the rest of your life: you are an adopted child of God, a co-heir with Christ.

"'What is a Christian?' The question can be answered in many ways, but the richest answer I know is that a Christian is one who has God as Father."

-J.I. Packer

A Disciple
of Christ

BY DONALD S. WHITNEY

I f you wanted to become a professional baseball player, how would you make that happen? Or, if you wanted to be a professional singer, how would you pursue that dream?

You would start the way anyone starts to work toward such goals: disciplined practice. In order to become a major league ballplayer, you would need to hone your skills daily. To become a professional vocalist, you'd practice every day, even though it meant forsaking other things you'd enjoy.

Some days, though, it's difficult. The discipline becomes drudgery. The solution on those days is to remember what you're trying to become and to recall the vision that motivated you in the first place. Remembering the goal gives you direction, and the direction prevents drudgery.

The Christian life is no different.

QUESTIONS:

What is something you've worked hard for in life? What was it that kept you motivated and disciplined?

_____

_____

_____

_____

The promise

As someone who has turned from sin and put your trust in Jesus, you are now a disciple of Christ. For all who follow Jesus, there are glorious promises that you will one day be conformed into his image (Romans 8:29). One day, you will be made like him (1 John 3:2). That won't be until you see him face-to-face, but it's a guarantee straight from God's Word. You're already a disciple of Christ, and you are becoming someone who will be completely transformed into Christ's image.

Pursuing that vision of Christlikeness is a lifelong endeavor, and the means of that pursuit is discipline, discipline for the purpose of godliness. By God's grace and the help of his Spirit, we work hard to become what God says we'll become. Have you ever noticed the relationship between the words "disciple" and "discipline"? That's no accident. God expects disciples of Christ to discipline themselves:

"Strive for peace with everyone, and for the holiness without which no one will see the Lord" (Hebrews 12:14).

That word "strive" is important. Christians must strive and work for personal holiness. Why? Because without it we will not "see the Lord." Even though we are saved by God's grace and the work he has done for us in Christ, we can't coast our way into eternal life. We must pursue godliness.

So, if God has said that ultimately all in Christ will be made like him – and that the evidence of this will be shown in our growth in godliness now – then how do we do that?

The answer comes in 1 Timothy 4:7: "Train yourself for godliness."

Discipleship through (spiritual) discipline

God calls all disciples of Christ to train for godliness. The Bible says that physical training is of some value, but training for godliness is of eternal value (1 Timothy 4:8). The way we train for godliness is through what have been called the spiritual disciplines. These disciplines are the means to godliness. Just like those who train to be ballplayers or singers, we don't practice spiritual disciplines just to practice, but for a much bigger purpose. The spiritual disciplines are a God-given means to godliness.

God uses many things to make us more like Jesus, including external things we can't control like people and circumstances. The spiritual disciplines, however, are different because they work from the inside out. Moreover, unlike many of the other ways God influences us toward Christlikeness, we have a lot of choice over how devoted we'll be to practicing the spiritual disciplines.

When I talk about the spiritual disciplines, I mean practices taught or modeled in the Bible. There may be other good activities you enjoy and find helpful, but God knows the ones that are best for making us more like Jesus. And he has revealed these to us in the Bible.

The biblical spiritual disciplines include prayer, fellowship, service, solitude, fasting, worship, and more. One way to divide these disciplines is into the categories "personal" and "interpersonal." The personal disciplines are the ones we practice alone: like private prayer, solitude, and keeping a spiritual journal. The interpersonal disciplines are the ones we practice with others – especially the church – like fellowship, service, and worshiping God with his people. And some disciplines are both: for example, God tells us to worship him privately and with others.

Of all the disciplines, though, there are two that are more important than the rest: Bible intake and prayer.

Bible intake

No spiritual discipline is more important than the intake of God's Word. There simply is no healthy Christian life apart from a diet of the milk and meat of Scripture. We find in Scripture how to live in a way that is pleasing to God. If we want to be godly, we must know the Word of God – intimately.

Jesus emphasized the importance of this when he said, "Man shall not live by bread alone, but by every word that comes from the mouth of God" (Matthew 4:4). It is through the regular, personal intake of the Bible that we come to know God better, understand his will for our lives, experience God's transforming presence, and much more.

1. Hearing God's Word

If we don't discipline ourselves to hear God's Word regularly, we may only hear it accidentally, just when we feel like it, or we may never hear it at all. For most of us, disciplining ourselves to hear God's Word means developing the practice of steadfastly attending a New Testament church where the Word of God is faithfully preached.

2. Reading God's Word

Here are three practical suggestions for consistent success in Bible reading:

First, find the time. Did you know that in no more than 15 minutes a day you can read through the Bible in less than a year? And yet the majority of Christians never read the Bible all the way through in their whole life. Second, find a Bible reading plan. It's no wonder that those who simply open the Bible at random each day soon drop the discipline. Keep a record of which books you've read. That way, regardless of how long it takes, or in what order they're read, you'll know when you've read every book in the Bible. The appendix of this book includes some suggestions for finding a good plan.

Third, find at least one word, phrase, or verse to meditate on each time you read (more on meditation below).

3. Studying God's Word

The basic difference between Bible reading and Bible study is simply a pencil and a piece of paper. Write down observations about the text as you read and record questions that come to your mind. Learn to use the cross-references in your Bible and by them compare verses in the passage you are reading with related passages elsewhere in the Bible. Experience the joy of discovering biblical insights firsthand through your own Bible study!

4. Memorizing God's Word

Memorizing Scripture will benefit you in a number of ways: it will give you more spiritual victories – you will make Scripture available for the Holy Spirit to take and ignite within you when it's needed. It will strengthen your faith because it repeatedly reinforces the truth, often just when you need to hear it again. And it will prepare you for unexpected witnessing or counseling opportunities that come your way.

The apostle Paul calls us to let the Word dwell in us richly (Colossians 3:16), so we should seek to be like the psalmist who said, "I have stored up your word in my heart, that I might not sin against you" (Psalm 119:11).

07

QUESTIONS:

What does your Bible intake look like right now? How could you grow in this discipline? What are some goals you can set to hear, read, study, and memorize the Scriptures more faithfully?

_____

_____

_____

_____

_____

_____

_____

_____

Prayer

Prayer is the next most important spiritual discipline. As disciples of Christ, we have access to the throne room of God through prayer. Every time we pray, we come before the Father in the name of Jesus.

Remarkably, God hears every prayer of his children, even when our prayers are weaker than a snowflake. To be like Jesus, we must pray. Jesus himself prayed all the time, sometimes through the night (Luke 6:12), so to pursue Christlikeness means we must pray.

The expectation to pray is not only a divine summons, but also a royal invitation. My wife, Caffy, expects me to call her when I travel. But that expectation is an expectation of love. She requires that I call because she wants to hear from me. God's expectation that we pray is like that. His command to pray is a command of love. In his love, he desires to communicate with us and to bless us.

Often we don't pray because we doubt that anything will actually happen. Or we don't sense that God is near to us when we pray, so we don't do it. Or we don't think we have all that many reasons to pray. Or perhaps we don't pray because we don't really know how.

Because of this, many of us need to learn how to pray. A child of God gradually learns to pray in the same way that a growing child learns to talk. We can learn by praying with others, praying on our own, reading about prayer, and studying the prayers of Scripture.

No matter what, the pursuit of God in prayer is worth it. It is worth any amount of frustration and discouragement. Don't let the enemy tempt you to become silently cynical about God's willingness and ability to answer. Let a love for God cause you to prevail in prayer.

QUESTIONS:

What does your prayer life look like? How can you grow in this discipline? Are there times of day when you can include prayer, even if briefly?

_____

_____

_____

_____

_____

A problem

I've been either a pastor, professor, or both for about 25 years, and in my experience there is an almost universal problem with both Bible intake and prayer.

With the intake of Scripture, even the most devoted readers will read a few chapters of their Bible, and then close it when they're done and not remember a single thing. It's not because they're not smart. No, it's not an issue of ability, but of method.

Reading Scripture is important because it exposes us to Scripture. But we want not merely to be exposed to Scripture, we want to absorb it. And that happens through meditation on (not just reading) the Bible. Meditation is simply lingering on something you've read, for even a minute. That will change the way you receive the Word. It's through meditation on Scripture that we begin to sense the experience with God and transformation of life that we hope for when we come to the Bible.

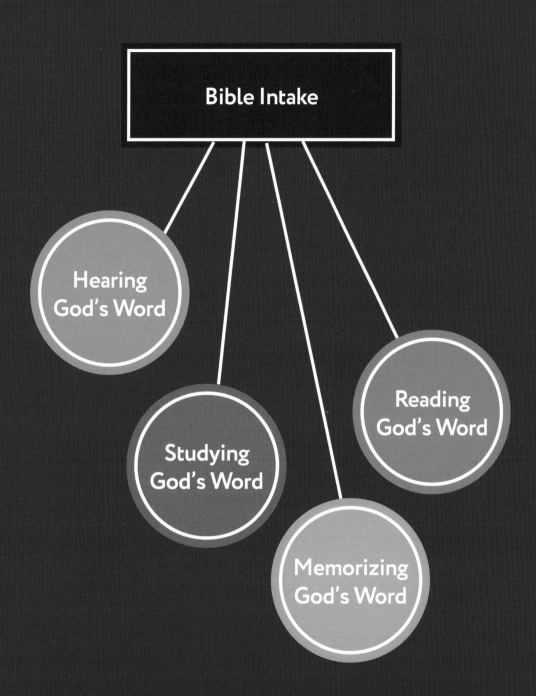

So even if you have only 10 minutes, read for five minutes and meditate for five. Read a big section (such as a whole chapter) and meditate on something small in that passage, such as one verse or phrase.

There's a problem with prayer, too: we end up saying the same things over and over and get bored. It's not wrong to pray about the same things repeatedly, for usually our lives consist of pretty much the same things from one day to the next. The problem is saying the same things about them, for eventually that becomes boring. And when you're bored with prayer, you don't pray. There's a simple solution: pray the Bible. Pray through a passage of Scripture, like one of the Psalms, and pray about what you read there.

For example, you could pray through Psalm 23. You read the first verse, "The Lord is my shepherd." Then you pray something like, "Lord, I thank you that you are my shepherd. You've shepherded me all my life. Would you shepherd my family today, guide them into your ways and away from the ways of the world? Lord, shepherd me through this upcoming decision I have to make. I don't want to be foolish, but follow you." And you would continue praying about whatever comes to mind as you read those words, "The Lord is my shepherd."

Then, when nothing else comes to mind, go to the next line. If you don't understand it, go on to the next line. If you understand the next one well, but nothing comes to mind to pray about, go on to the next line. Pray until you've run out of time, or until you're at the end of the psalm.

When you pray the Bible like that, you won't end up saying the same things over and over again. It's so simple that anybody can do it.

REFLECTION:

Use the space here to practice praying Scripture. Use this verse and write out prayers that relate to the verse.

"Whatever you do, work heartily, as for the Lord and not for men, knowing that from the Lord you will receive the inheritance as your reward. You are serving the Lord Christ" (Colossians 3:23-24).

_____

_____

_____

_____

Commit yourself

We all have reasons to ignore the disciplines, though, don't we? We're busy and there's homework or something else to do.

But the reality often is that we simply have not made the spiritual disciplines a priority. It's not that we fail to practice the disciplines only because we have no time — our devotion to TV, Facebook, and Netflix prove that we regularly do have some discretionary time. Rather, it's more often that we do not practice the spiritual disciplines because we do not plan to.

So you've got to be intentional with your time. If you have no plan in place, it won't happen. You can't just say, "I'll practice the disciplines when I have time." You'll just keep pushing it off. So make a plan and a schedule, or you will set yourself up for disappointment and discouragement.

Commit yourself now to practicing the spiritual disciplines, especially to Bible intake and prayer. God will change you through the disciplines, and you will be transformed more and more into Christlikeness.

As a disciple of Christ, that's what life is all about.

"All my weak days have a common cause - I have neglected communion with God through my neglect of the Scriptures and prayer."

- Paul Washer

A Member of the Body

WHY MEMBERSHIP MATTERS

BY JONATHAN LEEMAN

for years I called myself a Christian, but I'm not sure I really was one. I believed that Jesus died and rose again for the forgiveness of my sin. Once in a while I read the Bible that my grandma had given me. And once in a while I attended either church or a student fellowship. Never, however, did I commit to a church.

Being around Christians embarrassed me. I was arrogant. I was self-sufficient. And I wanted to pursue my favorite sins. So I did. With gusto.

All and all, you might have called me a nominal Christian — a Christian in name only. I had been baptized, but my life looked pretty much like the world.

If someone had told me, "You cannot call yourself a Christian, live like this, and refuse to join a church," I probably would not have listened. I didn't have ears to hear. I wanted the benefits of salvation, but to continue living exactly the way I wanted to live.

Suppose then someone read a Bible passage like one of these to me:

Let us "not neglect to meet together...For if we go on sinning deliberately after receiving the knowledge of the truth, there no longer remains a sacrifice for sins" (Hebrews 10:25-26).

"No one born of God makes a practice of sinning" (1 John 3:9).

"By this all people will know that you are my disciples, if you have love for one another" (John 13:35).

Probably, I would have felt a little worried, but then I would have deceived myself and explained the verse away by saying something like "Well, nobody's perfect" or "I can name a few Christians who I love."

Yet let's back up a step. How do we become a Christian? We turn away from our sin and trust in Christ's death and resurrection. We repent and believe. The Bible teaches that we are justified by grace alone through faith alone. This means that we don't do anything to earn salvation. It's a gift.

But the Bible also teaches that the grace and faith which justify are never alone. True faith works, you might say. True Christians show themselves to be Christians by loving God, fighting sin, and committing themselves to other believers. That's why Jesus says you know a tree by its fruit (Matthew 7).

QUESTIONS:

"Every healthy tree bears good fruit, but the diseased tree bears bad fruit. A healthy tree cannot bear bad fruit, nor can a diseased tree bear good fruit" (Matthew 7:17-18).

As you look at your life, what are some evidences of life and growth? Are you producing good fruit or bad fruit? If faith is the root, what are some of the fruits in your life?

_____

_____

_____

_____

Here is something exciting. God is so big and so powerful and so wonderful he takes natural-born sinners like you and me and makes us new. Can you believe it?! We don't change all at once. We're justified all at once, but we change little by little. Yet God really does change us. His Spirit is more powerful than the strongest of our weaknesses. And one of the most important ways he changes us is by giving us a new family and placing love in our hearts for them. That's the church.

So if someone tells me that God has made them new, but they are not walking in newness of life, it's hard for me to believe them. In the same way, if someone tells me that God has made them a member of Christ's body, his church, but they haven't actually joined a local church, it's hard for me to believe them.

Again, this is what we see in the Bible. When the people asked Peter what they must do to be saved, Peter replied, "Repent and be baptized" (Acts 2:38). Then we read, "So those who received his word were baptized, and there were added that day about three thousand souls" (v. 41). Added to what? Added to the membership of the church in Jerusalem. They were taking names and counting numbers.

Are you a Christian? If so, you need to be baptized into a church. That's the first step of the Christian life.

08

Using these verses, what are some reasons that not being part of a church makes the Christian life more difficult? Why is it not God's intention for us?

"Let us consider how to stir up one another to love and good works, not neglecting to meet together, as is the habit of some, but encouraging one another, and all the more as you see the Day drawing near" (Hebrews 10:24–25).

_____

_____

_____

_____

"If anyone says, 'I love God,' and hates his brother, he is a liar; for he who does not love his brother whom he has seen cannot love God whom he has not seen" (1 John 4:20). "By this all people will know that you are my disciples, if you have love for one another" (John 13:35).

_____

_____

_____

_____

> One of the most important ways he changes us is by giving us a new family and placing love in our hearts for them. That's the church.

Reasons why joining a church is important:

It's who you are.

It assures you of your salvation.

It's biblical.

It's a prerequisite for the Lord's Supper.

It publicly names you as an ambassador for King Jesus.

It's how you declare your highest allegiance.

It's how you embody and experience biblical images.

It's how you serve other Christians.

It's how you follow Christian leaders.

It enables church discipline.

It disciples us toward Christian maturity.

It builds a witness and invites the nations.

Let me give you twelve reasons why joining a church is critical to your soul and discipleship as well as to the witness of the gospel.

1. It's who you are. We join churches first and foremost because it's who we are — church members, or members of Christ's family. It's a part of our new identity. So become who you already are by joining a church. You are no longer just an "I." God has made you a "we."

2. It assures you of your salvation. When you join a church, the church is saying, "We believe that you understand the same gospel as we do, and we publicly affirm that you are a disciple of Jesus." And you are saying, "I will commit myself to this body's instruction and accountability so that I remain faithful. I will also commit to caring for others in this body."

All of this functions to assure us of our salvation. You might sometimes wonder if you are really a Christian. After all, you see all the pride, the vanity, the jealously, and all the other gunk in your heart. How good of God to give us brothers and sisters in Christ to point out where they do see evidences of grace in our life.

3. It's biblical. We should join a church as a matter of obedience. In addition to the passage in Acts mentioned above, think of Matthew 18 or 1 Corinthians 5 where Jesus and Paul, respectively, talk about being "removed" from a church (see Matthew 18:17; 1 Corinthians 5:2, 5, 12). How can someone be put "out" if they were never "in"? Church membership is the biblical pattern, and we should obey it.

4. It's a prerequisite for the Lord's Supper. The Lord's Supper is a meal for the gathered church, that is, for members. Listen to Paul again: "Because there is one bread, we who are many are one body, for we all partake of the one bread" (1 Corinthians 10:17). The one bread of the Lord's Supper shows that we are one body. The Supper, you might say, is a church-revealing activity. That's why Paul says in the next chapter, "When you come together to eat, wait for one another" (11:33). It's not something you take at home. It's something you take with members of your church.

5. It publicly names you as an ambassador for King Jesus. When a church affirms your profession of faith, they publicly affirm that you are a citizen of Christ's kingdom and an ambassador for Christ. They say that you represent Jesus. "Hey world, want to know Jesus is like? Look to this person!"

6. It's how you declare your highest allegiance. Not only does the church say, "This person is with Jesus," church membership is how you say, "I'm with Jesus." Joining a church through baptism and maintaining your fellowship through the Supper is how you make a public testimony.

QUESTIONS:

Of these first six reasons, which one hits home the most for you? Which one(s) have you never thought of before?

_____

_____

_____

_____

7. It's how you embody and experience biblical images. One scholar says there are over 90 images in the Bible for the church — images like bride, body, family, temple, people, flock, pillar, nation, branches, and so many more. Each one of these images has something to teach us about what life in the church is like. So when someone says, "What is church membership like?" you should answer, "Unlike anything else in the world! It's part family, part body, part bride, part pillar, part temple, and on and on." Wow!

8. It's how you serve other Christians. There are lots of "one another" commands in the Bible: love one another, serve one another, encourage one another, rebuke one another, submit to one another, and so forth. Which Christians on Planet Earth are you personally responsible for? Must you fulfill these commands for all the Christians in your country? In your city? In your neighborhood? Church membership answers that question. Primarily, we practice fulfilling all the "one another" commands in our local church.

9. It's how you follow Christian leaders. Hebrews 13:7 and 17 tells us to submit to our leaders. How do we know which leaders we should submit to (see also Acts 20:28; 1 Peter 5:2)? All the pastors in a country or city? No, we submit on a regular basis to the pastors of our church. Membership allows us to fulfill our biblical responsibility to our leaders.

10. It enables church discipline. Quick side lesson: what is church discipline? It's the process of speaking the truth in love to one another and correcting sin. You know how a math teacher teaches a lesson and then corrects any errors the students make? Church discipline is like that. It's part of how we grow in Christlikeness.

Sometimes, church discipline requires us to remove someone from membership in a church. We do that only when they refuse to let go of a significant and observable sin (something you can see or hear; we're not speculating about the heart) — when they are unrepentant. For instance, suppose a man calls himself a Christian, but he leaves his wife and children. His friends and the pastors should pursue him, and exhort him to return to his wife. If he doesn't return, eventually his church has no choice but to remove him from membership and participation in the Lord's Table. He's lying to himself, and he's lying about Jesus as a Jesus representative. Jesus would never abandon his wife! Read Matthew 18:15-17 and 1 Corinthians 5 where Jesus and Paul teach about this process.

When we remove someone from membership in the church, we are not saying we know for certain that he or she is a non-Christian. We are saying that we as a church can no longer affirm the person is a Christian. Paul says we should do this so that a person can be redeemed (1 Corinthians 5:5).

So we practice church discipline both because the Bible commands us to and for the sake of love: love for the sinner, love for other Christians, love for non-Christian witnesses, love for Christ. Can you exercise church discipline toward any Christian on the planet? No, church discipline should occur in the context of local churches where people know one another. That way it's done (hopefully) responsibly, wisely, and lovingly.

11. It disciples us toward Christian maturity. Church membership provides accountability for our Christians lives. In that sense, it helps to keep us on the path toward maturity and faithfulness. You might say it's God's discipling program.

12. It builds a witness and invites the nations. The boundaries drawn around the membership of a church yields a society of people which invites the nations to something better. It's God's evangelism program.

It's hard to follow Jesus in this world. The culture is like a strong river that will pull you into its current unless you have an island on which to stand, or, better, a boat that will travel up the current. A church is that island or boat.

QUESTIONS:

Christians are meant to live their lives differently than the surrounding world. What do you think are some of the ways a church helps you to do that? What features of church life — based on these reasons for joining a church — are different from what the world loves and values?

_____

_____

_____

_____

_____

I finally joined a healthy church after years of living like a nominal Christian. I won't get into all the details, but I think I became a Christian as a member of that church. No, that's not how it should ordinarily work. But that church loved me, cared for me, and taught me God's Word. And that made all the difference. My appetites and desires changed. No longer did I love the world most; I began to love God, God's Word, and God's people most.

So before you decide where to go to college, which job to take, where to move, which house to buy or apartment to rent, make sure there is a healthy church nearby. Your life and discipleship depend on it!

Things to look for in a church:

1. A healthy church <u>does</u> a number of things:

a. It builds itself up through God's Word and not the wisdom of the world.

b. It centers the weekly gathering around meaty biblical exposition (preaching through the text), the proclamation of the gospel, and the practical application of the gospel to all of life.

c. It practices church membership and encourages discipling.

d. It's led by a plurality of godly men for pastoring, praying, and preaching.

e. It loves God and it loves its neighbors in all sorts of practical ways.

2. A healthy church <u>is</u> a number of things:

a. It is hospitable, loving, and holy.

b. It speaks in a language the world can understand, but it lives distinctly from the world.

c. Members are welcoming, not suspicious of strangers, personally transparent, generous, quick to laugh but sober-minded, uninterested in evil but rejoice in the truth.

d. It's a place where old and young, rich and poor, educated and uneducated, one ethnicity and another find equal standing and the opportunity to serve.

"We need to give up trying to live the Christian life on our own. We need individually to covenant together with others to follow Christ."

- Mark Dever

A
Worshipper

BY DAN DEWITT

09

What should your new life in Christ look like now that you've experienced a life-transforming encounter with Jesus? Does following Jesus make that much of a difference in your day-to-day life? What should you do next?

In the following paragraphs, I want to take you on a quick survey of the book of Romans from a 30,000 feet view. We're going to fly over most of the apostle Paul's letter and land in chapter 12, where Paul urges Christians to be a living sacrifice. This is how he describes what it looks like to be a committed worshiper.

QUESTIONS:

When you hear the word "worship," what comes to mind?

_____

_____

_____

_____

_____

Romans 12:1 says that our "worship" is to present our "bodies as a living sacrifice, holy and acceptable to God." This suggests that God wants everything we do in our lives to be an act of worship. How does this change how you think of worship?

_____

_____

_____

_____

_____

101

Before we take off, consider this example of great sacrifice from history:

Operation Neptune

Operation Neptune was the codename for the naval operation of the Normandy invasion that took place on June 6, 1944. The overall Normandy plan was called "Overlord," which targeted five separate locations over a 60 mile stretch of Normandy beach: Utah, Omaha, Gold, Juno, and Sword Beach.

The plan involved 6,939 vessels including 4,126 landing crafts. It was the largest single day amphibious invasion of all time. It was a well planned, well executed, and hard fought victory, purchased with blood.

Among the first to navigate the beaches was a highly trained group of soldiers known as "Sappers." Sappers are combat engineers who detect and disable explosives. Sadly, and heroically, as the Sappers dodged bullets while clearing the way for soldiers, many of them discovered land mines when they stepped on them.

As journalist Tom Brokaw illustrates in his book, *The Greatest Generation*, the Sappers who survived the explosions would quickly self-administer a morphine shot that would enable them, in their dying moments, to point other soldiers towards safe terrain.

They planted themselves like trees and pointed others to the way of life. This kind of dutiful sacrifice deserves and demands our unqualified respect and gratitude. But what kind of mentality, what kind of character, what kind of devotion, undergirds such a commitment? This makes me think of the biblical description of what it means to be a living sacrifice.

> "I appeal to you therefore, brothers, by the mercies of God, to present your bodies as a living sacrifice, holy and acceptable to God, which is your spiritual worship." - Romans 12:1

It is to this end that I believe the apostle Paul devoted 11 chapters in his letter to the Romans. I consider the final verses of the eleventh chapter of Romans to be something like Paul's graduation speech for his students. After 11 chapters of describing grace, he concludes with a challenge before moving to more practical concerns in the remaining chapters.

He begins his challenge to his students this way, "Oh, the depth of the riches and wisdom and knowledge of God! How unsearchable are his judgments and how inscrutable his ways!" (Romans 11:33).

It's interesting that after Paul spends 11 chapters unpacking God's grace, he tells his audience that God's ways are unsearchable. He's making it clear that they might graduate from any number of things in their lives, just like you will graduate high school and college one day, but like them, you will never graduate from studying God's grace. You will never reach the bottom of it. Your life as a worshipper will be one of always learning more about grace.

That's why, even though God's ways are unsearchable, we are to treasure what we're able to study and understand in Scripture. Moses makes this clear when he writes, "The secret things belong to the Lord our God, but the things revealed belong to us and to our children forever" (Deuteronomy 29:29). The revealed things, the clear teachings of the Bible, are to be the focus of our lives.

This is, in many ways, the focus of the first 11 chapters of Romans. But before Paul moves to practical matters, it's as though he wants to give his students a heart check. He asks them three questions: "For who has known the mind of the Lord, or who has been his counselor? Or who has given a gift to him that he might be repaid?" (Romans 11:34-35).

These questions are simple: who has known God's mind? From whom did God seek advice? To whom is God indebted? These are rhetorical questions, which means the answers are implied or obvious. All the answers are negative.

Check it out:

Question 1: who has known God's mind?
Answer: no one.

Question 2: from whom did God seek advice?
Answer: no one.

Question 3: to whom is God indebted?
Answer: no one.

These rhetorical questions form the basis for the worldview of joyful sacrifice, of a life of worship. This is the reality of grace. This is the follower of Jesus coming face-to-face with his own inability set against the unending power of God. This is the realization that it is grace that has brought you thus far, that saved you, and it is grace that will lead you home.

Who has known God's mind? No one.
From whom did God seek advice? No one.
To whom is God indebted? No one.

To ask, "who has known the mind of the Lord," is to suggest that no one fully knows nor fully understands God's work. To ask, "who has been God's counselor," is to suggest that God is in need of no one's advice. To ask, "who has given God a gift and must be repaid," is to suggest, quite forcefully, that God is indebted to no one.

Because God has called you into a
relationship with Jesus Christ…

You are loved by God

You are purchased by the blood of the Son

You are sealed by the Spirit

You are kept for the glory of the Father

You are being sent

Living out the grace we have received

To graduate from Paul's school of theology, his students had to come face-to-face with their own insignificance. I believe that if we can't recognize our own insignificance, we can't be used by God. That is a theme of all of Scripture. God opposes the proud but gives grace to the humble.

We tend to want to boast about our accomplishments. Maybe just a humble brag. Maybe just a little bit of self-confidence. No. Paul says that we are completely indebted to God. His grace is what gave us new life.

It's almost as if Paul is saying, "Who do you think you are? God doesn't need you. He doesn't need me. He doesn't need us."

QUESTIONS:

In 1 Corinthians 4:7, Paul asks, "What do you have that you did not receive? If then you received it, why do you boast as if you did not receive it?" What are the answers to these questions? How do they relate to what Paul says in Romans 11?

_____

_____

_____

_____

_____

_____

_____

_____

> You are loved by God. You are purchased by the blood of the Son, sealed by the Spirit, and kept for the glory of the Father.

The reality is we can't cope with such insignificance apart from the grace of God. This is a great and beautiful picture Paul paints for us. He leads his students from these three rhetorical questions to a powerful statement. He leads them from insignificance to praise. He leads them to praise God for his abundant grace. In the next and final verse of chapter 11, Paul says, "For from him and through him and to him are all things. To him be glory forever. Amen" (Romans 11:36).

I'll tell you who you are. You are loved by God. You are purchased by the blood of the Son, sealed by the Spirit, and kept for the glory of the Father. You are called. And you are being sent.

That's why God called you into a relationship through Christ. That's why he forgave your sins. So that he could send you into the world to be a living testimony of his grace, not because you're so good but because he really is that good.

Every human sacrifice, like those I mentioned of brave soldiers in the beginning of the chapter, is still heroic, but very different from what we find in Scripture. Jesus' sacrifice not only saves our lives in the here and now, it purchases our salvation for the life to come. And this gift of salvation is from him, and it's for him, because to him, to Jesus, belongs all the glory.

A living sacrifice is living a life of worship

Paul gives a pointed application of these truths in the opening verses of Romans 12: "I appeal to you therefore, brothers, by the mercies of God, to present your bodies as a living sacrifice, holy and acceptable to God, which is your spiritual worship" (Romams 12:1-2).

This is the worldview of joyful sacrifice.

God loved you so much he spared not his own Son. What is the proper response to this? It is to die to yourself as a living sacrifice, to have your mind renewed through studying God's Word, and to live a life of worship.

So plant yourself like a tree and pour yourself out so that you might point others to the path of life. And never forget who you are. You are forgiven. You are called. You are sent. You are a worshipper. God has gloriously atoned for your sins and his sacrifice deserves and demands nothing less than our everything.

This is the gospel. And of this gospel, may you never be ashamed.

09

You've learned now that worship is about all of life, and that your commitment to Christ is to show up in your whole life. How does this affect the way you think about some normal things you do, like homework, chores, or a job? How do those things fit within the idea that all of life is worship? Are there areas of your life that need to be changed in order to be done as worship?

_____

_____

_____

_____

_____

_____

_____

_____

_____

_____

_____

"Worship is not one segment of the Christian life among others. Worship is the entire Christian life."

- John Frame

10

An Evangelist

TELL SOMEONE

BY KEVIN EZELL

10

One of my favorite stories in the Bible comes from the beginning of the Gospel of Mark. In this story, four men bring their paralyzed friend to Jesus for healing. But they couldn't get close to Jesus because the place was so crowded. So they climbed on top of the building, cut a hole in the roof, and lowered him down on his mat.

On their own, these guys couldn't do much to help their friend. But they knew enough to bring him to Jesus, and that's exactly what they did, even if it took cutting a hole in a roof. And Jesus didn't only heal the man physically. He also said to him, "Son, your sins are forgiven" (Mark 2:5).

There's an important message there for all of us: Jesus isn't asking us to convince people to become Christians. He doesn't expect us to be able to make such a compelling case that they can't resist believing. All he asks is that we bring people to him and he'll take care of the rest.

You might be young or new to the faith or both, but Jesus wants you to start bringing people to him right away.

Don't wait

Sometimes in life we allow ourselves to adopt an "I'll do that when" attitude. We say, "I'll get more serious about studying when I get to college," or "I'll start eating healthier when I graduate," or "I'll get more serious about my faith when I'm an adult."

But Jesus has called us to the right now, and when we're faithful to obey him, we will see great things happen.

My wife and I have a friend who teaches at a nearby public school. She is one of the sponsors of the Fellowship of Christian Athletes (FCA) group at the school. We will never forget when she told us about the coach at her school who became a believer because some students from that FCA group shared about Jesus with him. Today, when he tells people how he came to faith, he always mentions those FCA students.

What would have happened if those students had decided they were too young to talk to the coach about Christ?

A friend's daughter who attends public school shared a note of encouragement with her basketball coach one day and included Philippians 4:13, "I can do all things through him who strengthens me." The next time she stopped by her coach's office, the coach had hung that verse up on her wall. Then, the coach made it the theme verse for the team that season. It even ended up on the plaques each team member received at the end of season awards banquet!

Because a young believer followed God's nudge to write her coach an encouraging note, an entire team was inspired with a word from Scripture. And you can bet that verse led to a few conversations among families when the players brought their plaques home after that banquet!

Do you see what I mean about not waiting for God to use you right now?

QUESTIONS:

What are some ways you could take a bold step and initiate a conversation about the gospel? What are some good examples of peers who have taken a step of faith to tell someone about Christ?

_____

_____

_____

_____

10

God is always working

One of the exciting things about the Christian life is that God is always at work, everywhere, all the time. Sometimes we see evidence of that, but we're often unaware. I can't tell you how many times in my life I have looked at someone and thought, "they probably wouldn't be open to hearing about God." I know, it sounds terrible, but it's a trap we can easily fall into.

We see someone who looks like they have it all together. They dress just right, have a great car, have all the latest technology, and we can't imagine them needing God. But those kinds of judgments are way off. Some of the saddest, most unfulfilled people I have known lived in very nice neighborhoods and had a lot of great "stuff." Don't miss out on the opportunity to have a faith conversation with someone just because they look like they have it together by the world's standards. None of that is going to satisfy them and it certainly won't buy them a place in heaven.

At the same time, don't sell yourself short when it comes to your ability to tell people about God. Depending on your background, you might have the impression that only pastors or spiritual leaders can talk to people about Jesus. That's not the case. In fact, before he ascended into heaven, Jesus shared what is known as "The Great Commission" in Matthew 28:18–20. Essentially, Jesus gave a task to every believer (including me and you) to go and tell all people about him. He expected us to do that wherever we are.

> **One of the exciting things about the Christian life is that God is always at work, everywhere, all the time.**

Don't wait for God to use you right now

God is working everywhere and all the time

Jesus has given every believer the task to tell people about him

Get started by sharing your own journey of coming to know Jesus

10

Read Matthew 28:18–20. What does Jesus call his followers to do? What are some ways you can be doing this in your life?

_____

_____

_____

_____

_____

_____

_____

_____

Get started

Some people receive a special calling to be pastors or missionaries that travel across the country or across the world, but Jesus calls every believer to tell others about him.

So, how do you do that? To start, remember that if you understand enough to know you need forgiveness for your sins and Jesus as your Savior, then you know enough to tell others about him.

In fact, sometimes the most natural way to transition to that conversation is to share about your own spiritual journey. Let the person know how you came to the point of realizing that you needed Jesus. This will naturally lead to questions the person might have or opinions they have about faith and religion. The important thing is to point them toward the need we all have to seek forgiveness through Jesus. And be sure to tell them that Jesus is the only means of salvation — there is no other way.

There are many tools you can use when sharing your faith. I encourage you to check into some of them and see what fits you best. Ask your pastor or a friend who has been a believer for a while. I personally like a tool called the "Three Circles: Life Conversation Guide."

What's great about this tool is that it helps you make the transition from having a regular conversation to having a conversation about faith. You can download a free app by doing a search for "Life Conversation Guide" in the App Store or on Google Play. The app trains you how to use the tool. But there are many tools, you just need to use the one that is the right fit for you.

Most of all, remember that God's Holy Spirit is doing the real work of leading people to salvation. You might have first realized your need for Jesus when you were listening to a talk or reading a book. Regardless of what it was, the Holy Spirit worked through that person's words and led you to Jesus. God is made up of three persons — God the Father, God the Son, and God the Holy Spirit. So when you turned to Jesus, the Holy Spirit became part of your life as well. The Bible describes the Holy Spirit as a helper who helps us live the Christian life.

In Acts 1:8, Jesus said that believers will receive power from the Holy Spirit and that power helps us be "witnesses" for Jesus. A witness is simply someone who shares the truth about what he or she has seen and experienced.

Think about your family, your friends, neighbors, people at school or work. Just in those circles of people, there are dozens or hundreds who need to know Jesus like you do. Start praying for them. Pray that God would be at work in their lives, revealing himself to them. And pray for yourself — that you would be willing to share, willing to tell, willing to turn conversations toward Jesus.

REACTION:

Who are five people in your life who don't know Jesus? Write down their names and commit to praying for them every day for the next two weeks, and then look for opportunities to share the gospel with them.

1. _____

2. _____

3. _____

4. _____

5. _____

"Making disciples of Jesus is the overflow of the delight in being disciples of Jesus."

- David Platt

A

Reading Your Bible

BY TREY BRUNSON

I f we are going to consider a book on the topic of the basics of Christianity, it would seem most natural to consider the role of the Bible. While this is an appendix, there is nothing more important to this idea of beginning and growing as a Christians than reading the Bible.

Fewer things have been more beneficial to my spiritual growth than a systematic and rhythmic reading of the Scriptures, so my goal is to try and encourage you not only to read the Bible, but to grow in the Scriptures.

Pick a plan

It has been said, "a goal without a plan is just a wish." Ask most Christians what plan they have for reading their Bible and you will be surprised when you get a good answer. I don't mean that to condemn; I mean that to call you into action. We won't have a growing, encouraging, and healthy knowledge of the Bible without a plan and some determination.

If you think about reading in terms of consuming, imagine that you only ate a meal once a week on Sunday from 9-noon. How healthy could you be? Would you survive? That's how much Bible intake the majority of Christians get. Let that not be us. Get a plan that works for you and feast on all the riches of God's Word.

The easiest and best place to start is a standard "read your Bible in a year plan." Ligonier Ministries has a great list of these types of plans, and they are the simplest place to start. They are all formatted differently but with the basic idea of having you read a few chapters a day. Some of them are five days of reading with two days off, and some have you reading all seven days of the week. Some are a straight read from Genesis to Revelation, some are chronological, and some are a hybrid where you read from the OT, NT, and Psalms each day.

Pick a plan and begin to think through how you can get this rhythm into your daily schedule.

Pick a partner

I haven't seen most Bible reading plans focus on this, but I find choosing a partner for your reading to be crucial to the process of growing in discipline and grace. It's not only a form of accountability, but you will find that having another pair of eyes reading along with you helps you see things you might not have seen and gives you an outlet for processing passages that might not make sense. Who is close to you in your life? Proximity is a real blessing when it comes to discipleship or discipline because it removes a lot of the barriers and difficulties that come with chasing someone or hiding things.

Next, I would challenge you to consider someone who is either struggling in their knowledge of the Bible or has no knowledge of the Bible. I asked a friend of mine who was a Jewish atheist to read the Bible with me a few years ago. Keith seemed intrigued, but after three days had already given up because he couldn't understand Genesis. It gave me a huge opportunity to share about his heritage as a Jew with him, to explain Hebrew poetry to him, and to lay out the gospel to him.

Lastly, consider someone who is at the opposite end of life from you. If you're younger, consider asking a senior adult in your church to read with you. Cross-generational conversations are vital to growing. We need each other and we need to find real ways in the church to pass on what has been handed down. It will no doubt be a challenge, but it will also be a great joy.

Paul says that we are to "encourage one another and build one another up" (1 Thessalonians 5:11). We can graciously sharpen each other like iron. A partner will help you stay the course, but will also graciously walk with you when it's hard. Don't avoid the joy of a relational life. Use something like the pursuit of a discipline to grow together in order to go further.

Pick a place and time

I have heard my dad for years share stories about George W. Truett and W.A. Criswell, the pastors who led First Baptist Church Dallas for 100 years. Criswell is famous for saying, "Give your mornings to the Lord," and Truett is famous for staying up until 2 or 3 AM in the study. Both men were right. Find your time that works for you. I would say make sure you have a good 30 minutes to an hour in a place you can focus.

On normal days, I try to get up round 6 or 6:30 and carve out time before our boys get up. I sit at the kitchen table instead of a couch, or I just come in early and sit at my desk where I know I will have a quiet environment to read in.

The idea is that you be intentional about focusing on what you are doing. I cannot tell you how many times I have read a page in a book, only to get to the end and wonder what in the world I just read. Sometimes the difference is subject matter, but sometimes the difference is when you read, where you read, and how you read.

Pick some tools

Don't just read, study the Scriptures. Really dig in to know what you're reading about. A study Bible can help with this by having notes for you, but some of this just requires effort on your part. Before you read Samuel, Kings, and Chronicles, print out a chart that shows you the kingdoms of Israel and Judah with the kings, their dates, and whether or not they were good or bad. I tape one of these in the front of my Bible when I am reading through this section so that I know who I am reading about and where they fit in the history of Israel. You can do the same thing with the Judges and follow through that confusing period more easily as well.

Another area that requires some work is the prophets. You can also print out a chart of the prophets that tells you if they are speaking to Israel or Judah and whether that is pre, mid, or post exile. That helps you understand who the prophet is speaking to and why. A little bit of effort like that will help you make sure that you know what you are reading.

Read your Bible. Read regularly, with discipline, and with focus, because you can. You can know God more clearly and confidently by daily disciplining yourself to meet with him in the living pages of the Bible. Read your Bible because hope, strength, wisdom, and grace are kept there for you and every situation that you could ever find yourself. Read your Bible because there you will encounter significant stories that can change your life.

Read your Bible because there you see Jesus glorified and exalted as the object of your affection.

In the words of Charles Spurgeon, "ought you not to be profound in your knowledge of the words of God, so that you may be able to quote them readily when you would solve a difficulty, or overthrow a doubt? Since 'He hath said' is the source of all wisdom, and the fountain of all comfort, let it dwell in you richly, as 'A well of water, springing up unto everlasting life.' So shall you grow healthy, strong, and happy in the divine life."

Randall Breland serves in the central office as the director of communications at Crossings. He is pursuing a Ph.D. in Old Testament at Southern Seminary. Randall and his wife, Bethany, have two daughters.

Trey Brunson serves as the director of development for Crossings Ministries. He is pursuing his master of divinity from Southern Seminary and wrapping up his first film project, "Run the Race." Trey and his wife, Rachael, have three children.

Paul Chitwood is the executive director of the Kentucky Baptist Convention. He has served in a variety of roles, including pastor of a number of churches since 1993 and as the president of the Kentucky Baptist Convention in 2005–06. Paul and his wife, Michelle, have three children.

Matt Damico is associate pastor of worship at Kenwood Baptist Church in Louisville, Kentucky. He and his wife, Anna, have two daughters.

Dan DeWitt is associate professor of applied theology at Cedarville University and director of the Center for Biblical Apologetics and Public Christianity. He's the author of *Christ or Chaos* and *Jesus or Nothing*. Dan and his wife, April, have four children.

Kevin Ezell serves as the president of the North American Mission Board, which works to reach North America through evangelism and church planting. Prior to becoming president of NAMB, he served as senior pastor of Highview Baptist Church in Louisville, Kentucky for 14 years. Kevin and his wife, Lynette, have six children.

Greg Gilbert is the pastor of Third Avenue Baptist Church in Louisville, Kentucky. He's written several books, including *What Is the Gospel?* and *Who Is Jesus?* Greg and his wife, Moriah, have three children.

Kevin Hall is the director of programming and The Hub: For Youth and Family Ministries at Crossings. He has been involved in youth and college ministry for over 25 years and just finished his Ph.D. in systematic theology at Southern Seminary. Kevin and his wife, Ayemi, have one son.

James M. Hamilton Jr. is professor of biblical theology at Southern Seminary and the pastor of Kenwood Baptist Church in Louisville, Kentucky. He's the author of numerous books, including *God's Glory in Salvation through Judgment: A Biblical Theology* and *What Is Biblical Theology: A Guide to the Bible's Story, Symbolism, and Patterns*. James and his wife, Jill, have five children.

Jonathan Leeman serves as editorial director for 9Marks. He has written a number of books, including *Political Church: The Local Assembly as Embassy of Christ's Rule*. He edits the *9Marks Journal* and series of books. He also serves as an elder at the Capitol Hill Baptist Church in Washington, D.C. Jonathan and his wife, Shannon, have four daughters.

Donald S. Whitney is professor of biblical spirituality at Southern Seminary. He's the author of many books, including *Spiritual Disciplines of the Christian Life* and *Praying the Bible*. Donald and his wife, Caffy, have one daughter and a grandson.

Designer: Morgan Carter is a graphic designer located in Louisville, KY. She enjoys working as a freelance designer for organizations across the Southeast. Morgan and her husband Zach serve at Cedar Creek Baptist Church in Louisville.

We exist to proclaim the Gospel and to see God transform lives, grow leaders, and partner with the church to the glory of Christ. We are a ministry based in Louisville, Kentucky that offers camps, conference centers, retreats, missions trips, and resources.

Our 600-acre Cedarmore Camp and Conference Center is located in the rolling hills of Bagdad, Kentucky just 45 minutes east of Louisville. Our 100-acre Jonathan Creek Camp and Conference Center is located on Kentucky Lake between Murray and Paducah, Kentucky.

Visit www.gocrossings.org to learn more about our biblically-focused camps, Christ-centered conference centers, and strategic missions trips to Haiti and other international destinations.

As our name suggests, our purpose is centered around youth and family ministry. We exist to equip, edify, and encourage the local church. Our heart is to see the bride of Christ thrive and flourish as they disciple kids, students, and families. We come alongside kids and student pastors, church leaders, parents, and students as they endeavor to grow in Christ and navigate through the many challenges of life and ministry.

How do we accomplish our mission?
- We edify through our ministry-focused blogs, podcasts, and video series.
- We encourage through our array of digital and print resources that we make available to you.
- We equip through our veteran ministry coaches, youth and children's ministry specialists, focused conferences, and training events.

Visit www.youthandfamilyhub.org for more information, to access our resources, to request a speaker, or to contact one of our regional ministry specialist.